Copyright © 2018 by MJ Stevens
Artwork © 2018 by Jessica Volpe

All rights reserved. No part of this book may be reproduced or used in any manner without written permission of the copyright owner. For information and media inquiries address: publishing@deadendroad.co.

First edition 2019

Book design by Bill Stevens III
Illustrations and cover by Jessica Volpe

ISBN (hardcover): 978-1-7332690-0-1
ISBN (ebook): 978-1-7332690-1-8

Marigold Street Press
an imprint of DeadEndRoad Media
www.deadendroad.co

# Fred's First Adventure

by
MJ Stevens

illustrated by
Jessica Volpe

Fred sailed across the ocean on a great big boat.

At first he wasn't quite sure if it would float.

The ocean breeze was soft and warm.

The sun was out, the boat safe from storms.

Fred didn't know how long he should stay.

He came from so very far away.

Soon Fred saw the beach made of sand.

Then he knew his adventure would be grand.

There were lots of new things to see.

And there were many different kinds of trees.

Fred made a friend at a place called the zoo.

He didn't want this day to be through.

Fred and his friend Denise walked along the river.

They shared ice cream that made their teeth shiver.

Fred explored the city with his new friend.

They watched the sunset together
at the day's end.

When night came Fred took a nice rest.

Tomorrow would be the start of a brand new quest.

*For Denise,*

*Thank you for your love, your laugh, and for introducing us to Fred.*

# About the Author

MJ Stevens is a pre-school teacher from Pittsburgh, Pennsylvania. Growing up she and her sister had a fascination with koalas, or "Freds," as they called them.

MJ has three children and two cats. She now resides in New Jersey with her family and growing collection of "Freds."

For more adventure, visit MJ and Fred at mjstevens.net.

For readings, contact MJ at mj@mjstevens.net or publishing@deadendroad.co.

# About the Illustrator

Jessica Volpe is a painter and illustrator of children's stories. She has always loved to draw and paint and has never wanted to be anything other than an artist.

She grew-up in Toronto and now lives San Diego, California with her husband and daughter. Besides children's books, her work also appears in galleries around Toronto and California.

You can see more of her work at:

www.jessicavolpe.com

CPSIA information can be obtained
at www.ICGtesting.com
Printed in the USA
BVHW092224120819
555663BV00023B/2148/P